scrapbook of memories™
for my
SON

MADE ESPECIALLY FOR

FROM

DATE

INTEGRITY®
PUBLISHERS

TABLE OF CONTENTS

HOW TO CREATE *Your Scrapbook of Memories*™

Congratulations! You have found the perfect gift for your son! Just add memories, and you have a one-of-a-kind keepsake that will be treasured for a lifetime.

As you browse the pages of this scrapbook, think back over precious memories and unforgettable moments. As you fill each page with your thoughts, prayers, and remembrances, you are creating a customized token of love that can be enjoyed for years to come.

1. Look back over the special times you've had with your son, and record your memories with the help of the prompts provided on each page. (Unsure of some of the details? No problem! Save those prompts as a special opportunity to finish creating the scrapbook with the help of your son.)

2. Gather favorite photographs, and place them in the spaces provided.

3. Write a personal letter to your son in the space provided.

4. Tear out this page.

5. Save this Scrapbook of Memories for that special occasion, and then enjoy special moments along with your son as you recall all of the precious memories you've shared together.

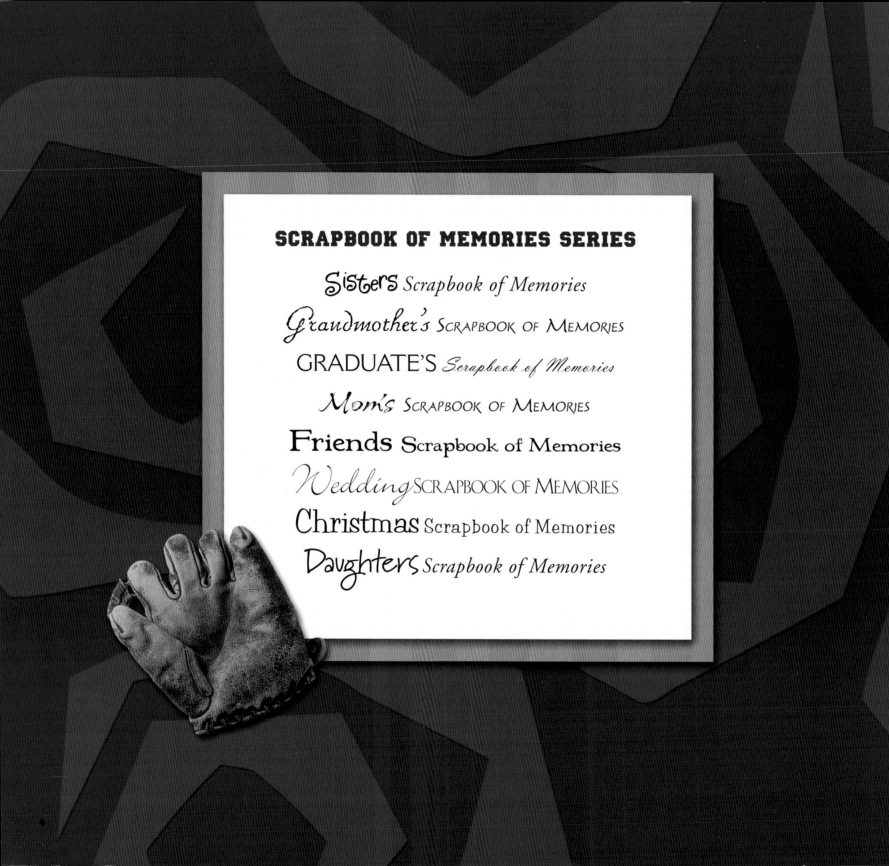

SCRAPBOOK OF MEMORIES SERIES

Sisters Scrapbook of Memories

Grandmother's SCRAPBOOK OF MEMORIES

GRADUATE'S *Scrapbook of Memories*

Mom's SCRAPBOOK OF MEMORIES

Friends Scrapbook of Memories

Wedding SCRAPBOOK OF MEMORIES

Christmas Scrapbook of Memories

Daughter's Scrapbook of Memories

A letter to my **SON**

Your FAMILY TREE

Your Mother's Family

Mom

Name _____

Date of Birth _____

Place _____

Your Maternal Grandparents

Name _____

Date of Birth _____

Aunts and Uncles

_____
_____
_____

Cousins

_____
_____
_____

Your Father's Family

Dad

Name _____

Date of Birth _____

Place _____

Your Paternal Grandparents

Name _____

Date of Birth _____

Aunts and Uncles

_____

_____

_____

Cousins

_____

_____

_____

Your family will be a
blessing to all people.
GENESIS 28:14 CEV

Some interesting history from your mother's family

May the LORD, the God of your
fathers ... bless you, just as
He has promised you!"
DEUTERONOMY 1:11 NASB

Mom

dad

Interesting history from your father's family

_____

_____

_____

_____

_____

_____

_____

_____

_____

_____

_____

_____

_____

_____

_____

_____

_____

_____

_____

The DAY You Were BORN

_____was born to

_____and_____

on_____at_____a.m./p.m.

Weight_____ Length_____

Hair Color_____ Eye Color_____

May your father and mother be glad;
may she who gave you birth rejoice!

PROVERBS 23:25 NIV

When I learned that I was expecting you

_____

_____

_____

_____

_____

My feelings the first time I held you

We brought you home to

Your siblings

We chose your name because

11

oh, BABY BOY!

Your baby quirks and early personality

_____

_____

_____

Your favorite lullaby

_____

_____

What made you happy

_____

_____

What made you cry

_____

_____

Baby's eating and sleeping habits

_____

_____

_____

I will praise You, for I am fearfully *and* wonderfully made.
PSALM 139:14 NKJV

A gallery of firsts:

Smile _____

Sit _____

Crawl _____

Steps _____

Words _____

Haircut _____

It's a Boy!

Beloved memories of your babyhood

_____
_____
_____
_____
_____
_____
_____
_____

TODDLER *Years*

Special memories of your toddler years

_____
_____
_____
_____
_____
_____
_____
_____

Your toddler temperament

_____
_____
_____
_____
_____
_____

Toddler Favorites

Toy

Game

Food

Pet

Book

TV show

Movie

People

Song

Bible story

Bedtime story

CHILDHOOD

I loved to watch you when

_____
_____
_____
_____
_____
_____
_____
_____
_____
_____

But Jesus said, "Let the little children come
to Me, and do not forbid them;
for of such is the kingdom of heaven."
MATTHEW 19:14 NKJV

Some of the funniest things
you ever said

_____
_____
_____
_____
_____
_____
_____
_____

Your best wonder-filled questions

_____
_____
_____
_____
_____
_____

Childhood Firsts

Learned to swim

Lost your first tooth

Learned to read

Learned to ride a bicycle

When you grew up,
you wanted to be

Just YOU & ME

When you and I spent time alone

_____
_____
_____
_____
_____
_____
_____
_____
_____

My nickname(s) for you

_____
_____
_____
_____

Mother-son time was special because
_____
_____
_____
_____
_____
_____
_____
_____
_____

My favorite times with you
_____
_____
_____
_____
_____
_____
_____

Just
YOU & DAD

Father-son time was important because

When you and your dad were alone

"I will be his father,
and he will be my son.
I will never take my love
away from him."
1 CHRONICLES 17:13 NIV

Dad's nickname(s) for you

The best times you and Dad had together

FAMILY *Life*

Our goals as a family

What family means to us

Our family motto

We spend time as a family

Our favorite family activities

_____
_____
_____
_____

"But as for me and my house, we will serve the LORD." JOSHUA 24:15 NASB

Our weekend activities

_____
_____
_____
_____

Family FAITH

Favorite family prayers

_____
_____
_____
_____
_____
_____
_____
_____
_____
_____
_____
_____
_____
_____

Our family spent time with God by

_____
_____
_____
_____
_____
_____
_____
_____

Blessed are the merciful

I'm eager to encourage you in your faith, but
I also want to be encouraged by yours.
ROMANS 1:12 NLT

Favorite family scriptures

The church you grew up in

You were baptized/dedicated

Family VACATIONS

Places our family vacationed

Mt. Rushmore

"The LORD your God will be
with you wherever you go."
JOSHUA 1:9 NIV

Your favorite family vacation

In the summertime, you

A family vacation nightmare

ALASKA

Special visits with family and friends

CHILD'S *play*

What you liked to do for fun

_____

_____

_____

Your special outings

_____

_____

Your most meaningful childhood achievement

_____

_____

_____

_____

_____

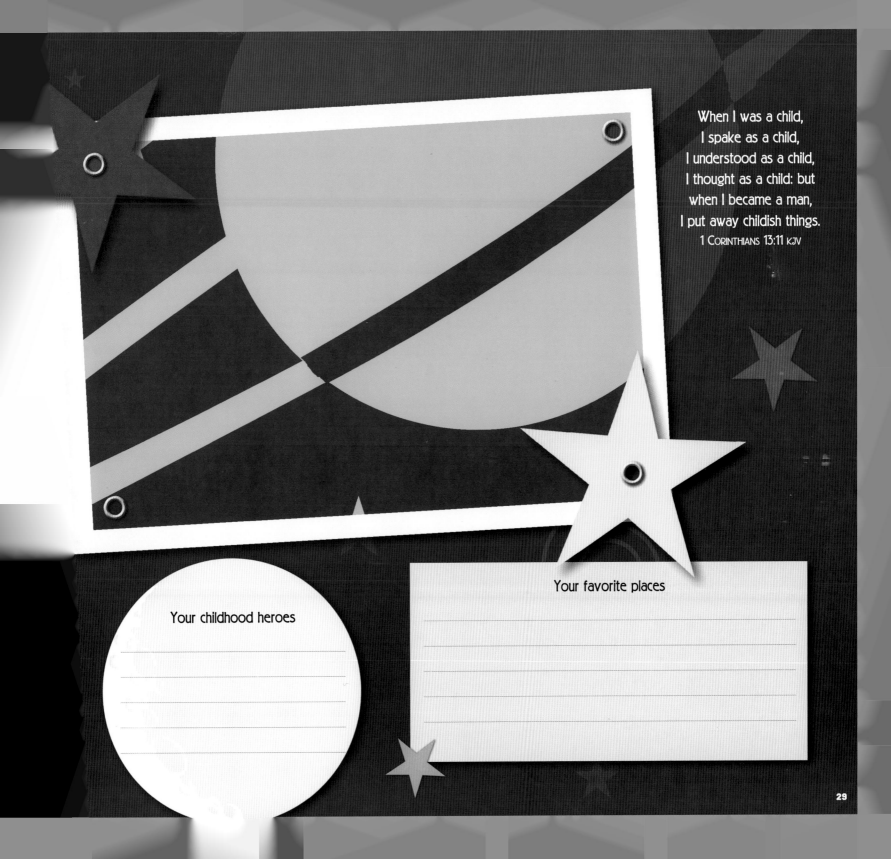

When I was a child,
I spake as a child,
I understood as a child,
I thought as a child: but
when I became a man,
I put away childish things.
1 CORINTHIANS 13:11 KJV

Your favorite places

Your childhood heroes

MESSY, MUDDY, MISCHIEF

Where you "explored" outdoors

_____

_____

_____

_____

_____

Be happy . . . while you are young, and let your heart give you joy in the days of your youth.
ECCLESIASTES 11:9 NIV

Your favorite way to get messy

Your favorite way to make noise

_____
_____
_____
_____
_____
_____

Mischief you created

_____
_____
_____
_____

ACTIVITIES

Lessons you took (Activity/Years)

_____

_____

_____

_____

_____

_____

Group activities (Activity/Years)

_____

_____

_____

_____

_____

Concerts/performances

_____

_____

_____

_____

A memorable event

Medals or awards
you won

SPORTS

Sports you played（Sport/Year）

_____

_____

_____

_____

_____

_____

_____

_____

_____

hey shall run, and not be weary;
d they shall walk, and not faint.

A game I will never forget

Why I loved to watch you play sports

Sports recognition you earned

FAVORITES

TV show

Movie

Music style

Song

Sport

Hobby

Book

Bible story

Color

"For where your treasure is,
there your heart will be also."
Luke 12:34 NASB

Pet

Candy

Possession

Ice cream flavor

Food

Place to go

TEEN *Life*

On the weekends, you

You and your friends enjoyed

Youth group events at church

Fashion trends

What was considered "cool"

Popular Hairstyles

How can a young man
keep his way pure?
By living according
to your word.
PSALM 119:9 NIV

Dance

Date

Driver's license (Date)

Car

Shaving

FRIENDSHIPS

A man *who has* friends must himself be friendly,
But there is a friend *who* sticks closer than a brother.
PROVERBS 18:24 NKJV

Your best childhood friend(s)

Your longest friendship

Your group of friends now

A time that I prayed for you and your friends

Good friends are a blessing from God

You are a good friend because

DATING & LOVE

Your first girlfriend

You started dating

Memorable parties, dances, or proms

_____

God teaches us that love

We love, because He first loved us.
1 John 4:19 NASB

BIRTHDAY
Celebrations

We liked to celebrate birthdays by

"We had to celebrate this happy day."
LUKE 15:32 NLT

Age

Age

Age

Your first birthday

Age

Memorable
BIRTHDAY PARTIES

Your best birthday parties

What we did

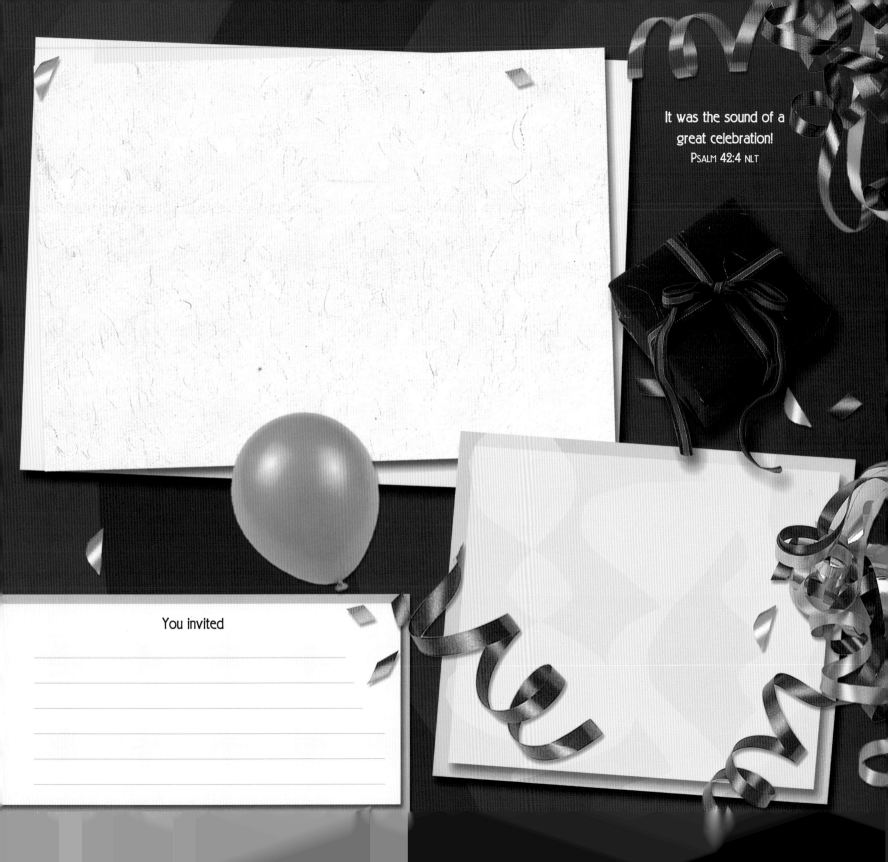

It was the sound of a
great celebration!
PSALM 42:4 NLT

You invited

HOLIDAY
Celebrations

NEW YEAR'S EVE
To celebrate the New Year, we

Our favorite New Year's Eve celebration

VALENTINE'S DAY
For Valentine's Day, we

The best valentine you ever gave me

Rejoice in the Lord always.
PHILIPPIANS 4:4 NIV

EASTER

We celebrated Easter by

_____

_____

_____

_____

Easter services we attended

_____

_____

We decorated Easter eggs

_____

_____

_____

HOLIDAY FUN

THE 4TH OF JULY

We celebrated the 4th of July by

_____

_____

_____

Our favorite fireworks display

_____

_____

HALLOWEEN

Your favorite Halloween costumes

Fun Fall activities

THANKSGIVING

We celebrated Thanksgiving with

Our family is thankful for

"Give thanks to the LORD, for his love endures forever."
2 CHRONICLES 20:21 NIV

Our traditional Thanksgiving meal

_____

_____

_____

_____

_____

Recipe Card

CHRISTMAS
Traditions

Christmas in our family means

_____
_____
_____
_____

Our family's Christmas traditions

_____
_____
_____
_____
_____
_____
_____
_____
_____

Glory to God in the highest,
and on earth peace, good will toward men.
LUKE 2:14 KJV

Every Christmas, we

_____

_____

_____

_____

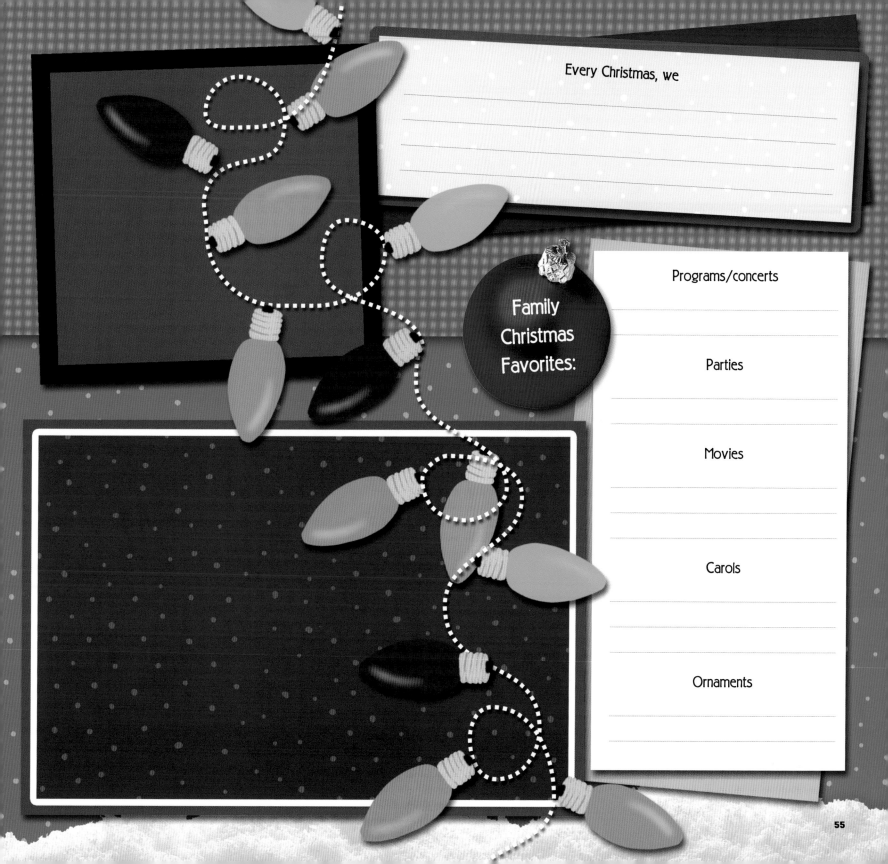

Family Christmas Favorites:

Programs/concerts

Parties

Movies

Carols

Ornaments

MERRY CHRISTMAS!

When we decorated the Christmas tree

On Christmas Eve, we

On Christmas Day, we

When we opened Christmas gifts

For unto you is born this day in
the city of David a Saviour,
which is Christ the Lord.
LUKE 2:11 KJV

Your favorite part of Christmas

PRESCHOOL & KINDERGARTEN

Since my youth, O God,
you have taught me,
and to this day
I declare your
marvelous deeds.
PSALM 71:17 NIV

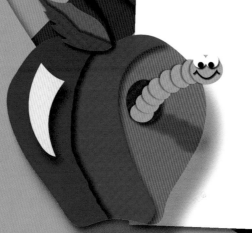

Preschools you attended (dates)

Kindergarten you attended (dates)

On your very first day of school, I

Your favorite part of school

Things you learned in Kindergarten

ELEMENTARY SCHOOL

School(s) attended

A B C D E F G H I J K L M N O P Q R S T U V W X Y Z

Best school friends

Favorite subject(s)

Favorite teacher(s)

1

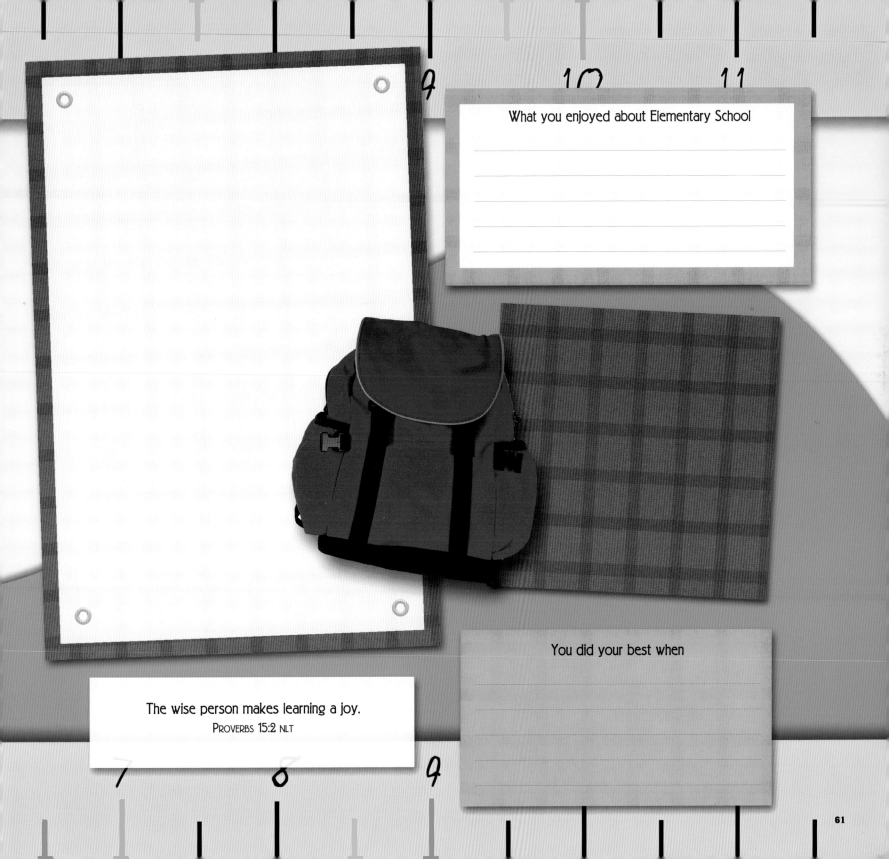

What you enjoyed about Elementary School

You did your best when

The wise person makes learning a joy.
PROVERBS 15:2 NLT

MIDDLE SCHOOL

School(s) attended

Best subject(s)

Favorite teacher(s)

Best school friends

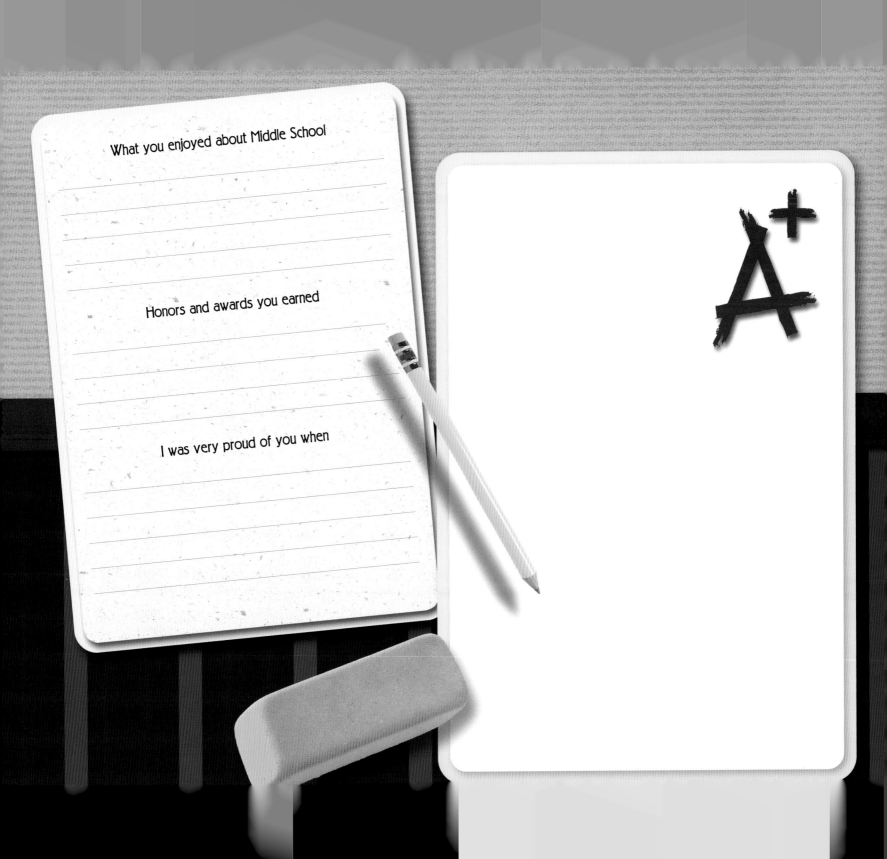

What you enjoyed about Middle School

Honors and awards you earned

I was very proud of you when

High SCHOOL

Best subject(s)

Favorite teacher(s)

GEOMETRY

$a = \pi r^2$

School(s) you attended

High School friends

I devoted myself to study and to explore by wisdom all that is done under heaven.

ECCLESIASTES 1:13 NIV

Awards and recognition

Best High School memories

HIGH SCHOOL *Highlights*

High School   Graduation date

Your High School Commencement Ceremony was at

Kanawha County Public Schools

Charleston High School
This Certifies that
David Jonathan Dupey
having completed the course of study prescribed by the Kanawha County Board of Education is hereby declared a graduate of this High School and is entitled to this
Diploma
Given by order of the Board of Education, in and for the County of Kanawha, at Charleston, West Virginia, June 9, 1984.

High School Highlights

COLLEGE

College(s) you attended

_____

_____

_____

During College you lived

_____

_____

_____

"Be strong and do not give up,
for your work will be rewarded."
2 CHRONICLES 15:7 NIV

Your major(s)

Your minor(s)

College friends

_____
_____
_____
_____

Jobs during College

_____
_____
_____
_____

UNIVERSITY

Your best memories of College

_____
_____
_____
_____
_____
_____
_____
_____
_____
_____

Our **RELATIONSHIP**

I love being your mom

_____
_____
_____
_____
_____
_____
_____
_____

When we're together, we like to

_____
_____
_____
_____

The best talk we've ever had

_____
_____
_____
_____
_____

I hope I will be remembered for

What you have taught me

I could have no greater joy
than to hear that my children
live in the truth.
3 JOHN 4 NLT

Favorite MEMORIES

It was so fun when

You made my day when

I laughed so hard when

I couldn't believe that you

I'll never forget the time

Life's
LESSONS

Things that came easy for you

BUMPS AHEAD

Trust in Him at all times.
PSALM 62:8 NKJV

Lessons you've learned the hard way

I was praying for you when

What I admire most about you

I will always be here for you

MOM'S *Advice*

Advice to you on . . .

What matters most

Faith

Growing older

"When you go through deep waters and great trouble, I will be with you . . . For I am the LORD, your God, the Holy One of Israel, your Savior."

ISAIAH 43:2-3 NLT

The best advice I've been given

Love

Parenting

Enjoying life

With
LOVE

My dreams for your future

I hope I have taught you

I see in you

My prayers for you

"The LORD make His face shine upon you,
And be gracious to you."
NUMBERS 6:25 NKJV

You are a wonderful son

Sons
scrapbook of memories™

Copyright © 2004 by Integrity Publishers
Published by Integrity Publishers
A division of Integrity Media, Inc.
5250 Virginia Way, Suite 110
Brentwood, TN 37027

HELPING PEOPLE WORLDWIDE
EXPERIENCE the MANIFEST PRESENCE of GOD

Scripture references are from the following sources:
The Holy Bible, New International Version (NIV). Copyright © 1973, 1978, 1984,
International Bible Society. Used by permission of Zondervan Bible Publishers.
The New King James Version (NKJV), © 1979, 1980, 1982, Thomas Nelson Publishers, Inc.,
Nashville, Tennessee 37214. The Holy Bible, New Living Translation (NLT), © 1996 Tyndale
House Publishers, Inc., Wheaton, Illinois 60189. New American Standard Bible (NASB),
© 1960, 1977 by the Lockman Foundation. The Contemporary English Version (CEV),
© 1991 by the American Bible Society. The King James Version of the Bible (KJV).
Used by permission. All rights reserved.

Guide Questions and Editorial Content by
Amy Koechel Smith

CONCEPT AND DESIGN BY KOECHEL PETERSON & ASSOCIATES, INC.

Printed in China.
04 05 06 07 RRD 9 8 7 6 5 4 3 2 1